The Kids' Book of
CHOCOLATE

The Kids' Book of
CHOCOLATE

by Richard Ammon

Atheneum   New York   1987

PICTURE CREDITS

Map on pages 8–9 and diagrams on pages 6 and 43 by Bruce Hiscock

Photographs:
Darrell Peterson: frontispiece, 12 (top) 16, 23, 25, 26, 28
36, 38, 40, 41, 42, 45, 46, 47, 59, 61, 65, 70
Penny Buzzard: 10
Bryson Leidich: 14
Courtesy of U.S.D.A.: 13
Courtesy of Public Relations Office, Hershey Foods Corporation: 30, 32, 35, 37

Excerpt on page 27 from *Charlie and the Chocolate Factory* by Roald Dahl used by permission.
Copyright © 1964, Alfred A. Knopf, Inc.
"Chocolate Cake" by Nina Payne reprinted by permission. From *All Day Long,* copyright © 1973,
Atheneum Publishers, Inc.
"Mother's Chocolate Valentine" from *It's Valentine's Day* by Jack Prelutsky, copyright © 1983
by Jack Prelutsky. Reprinted by permission of Greenwillow Books
(A Division of William Morrow & Company).
The first stanza of "The Reason I Like Chocolate," from *Vacation Time* by Nikki Giovanni,
copyright © 1980 by Nikki Giovanni, reprinted by permission of William Morrow & Company.
"Chocolate Milk" by Ron Padgett reprinted by permission of the author.
"Chocolate" from *Egg Thoughts and Other Frances Songs* by Russell Hoban, text copyright © 1964,
1972 by Russell Hoban, reprinted by permission of Harper & Row, Publishers, Inc.

Atheneum.
Macmillan Publishing Company. 866 Third Avenue, New York, NY 10022
Collier Macmillan Canada, Inc.

Type set by V & M Graphics, NYC. Printed and bound in the U.S.A. Designed by Mary Ahern
First Edition.   10 9 8 7 6 5 4 3 2 1

Library of Congress Cataloging-in-Publication Data

Ammon, Richard.
The Kids' Book of Chocolate

Bibliography: p. 72; Includes index.

SUMMARY: A history of chocolate, a discussion of the processing of cacao into chocolate products,
recipes, suggestions for related places to visit, and chocolate lore, jokes, and poems.
1. Chocolate—Juvenile literature. 2. Cookery (Chocolate)—Juvenile literature. [1. Chocolate] I. Title.
TX415.A46   1987   641.3'374   86-26564
ISBN 0-689-31292-X

Contents

For Jeannie

Acknowledgements

NO BOOK, even one this modest, is possible without the help of others, especially experts in the field. Therefore, I wish to extend special thanks to John Moon, vice-president, technical services, Godiva Chocolatier, recently retired, without whose help this book would not have been possible. I also want to thank Kervin Martin, Research & Development, Wilbur Chocolate Company, for his expert advice and help in photography. Thanks also go to Penny Buzzard, curator, Candy Americana Museum of Wilbur Chocolate Company, Inc., for her photographs of a cacao plantation and her gracious tour of the Candy Americana Museum. Thanks to Ray Sholly, manager of training, Hershey Plant, Hershey Chocolate Company and Brian Hermann, manager, media relations, Hershey Foods Corporation for arranging for photographs to be taken in the Hershey Chocolate Plant.

Most of all, I want to thank Marcia Marshall for helping me to see all the delicious possibilities.

Chocolate! Chocolate! Chocolate

DO YOU PAUSE when you pass the candy counter in a department store or mall? Does your mouth water just smelling the chocolaty aroma? Do you carefully unfold the foil on each piece of chocolate as if you were inspecting a treasure? Do you break off small bites, letting that wonderfully luscious chocolate smother your taste buds? If you treat chocolate like a rare gem, then you are upholding a tradition begun by the early Aztecs and Spaniards.

Archaeologists believe that the Mayan Indians of Central America cultivated cacao trees as early as the seventh century. Yet it was not until his fourth voyage to America in 1502 that Columbus became the first European to drink chocolate. He was not impressed. That may have been because it had a bitter taste, nothing like the chocolate drink you had for breakfast or lunch. Besides, Columbus was probably more interested in discovering gold and a new route to India than in sipping an awful-tasting beverage.

Instead, it was Hernando Cortés who introduced Europeans to what the Aztec Indians of Mexico called *Chocolatl*. It was not because chocolate now tasted any better. The chocolatl Montezuma treated Cortés to was probably as strong and bitter as ever. But Cortés was fascinated with the golden goblets used to serve the drink.

3

He was also intrigued with the Aztecs' idea of using cocoa beans as money. It cost, for example, ten beans for a rabbit and one hundred beans for a slave. There were even reports of counterfeit money—beans filled with dirt!

Cortés might have imagined money growing on trees. So wherever he explored, he planted cacao trees, hoping to become rich. As far as we know, the king of Spain preferred coins. Thanks to Cortés, cacao trees are found throughout Central America and Africa.

Hernando Cortés introduced Europeans to chocolatl.

4

This old print shows native Americans grinding chocolate beans and making it into cakes.

One reason the Aztecs treated Cortés so well was that they thought he might be Quetzalcoatl, one of their gods. The Aztecs believed Quetzalcoatl had brought cacao seeds from the Garden of Life for them. That may be why the Aztecs thought chocolate was a divine drink.

The Aztecs made chocolatl by roasting cocoa beans in clay pots. Then, on a concave stone, called a metate, they ground the beans with another stone, called a mona, producing a paste they formed into cakes. When the Aztecs wanted some chocolatl, they broke off a piece of cake, dissolved it in water, and whipped the

A molinet.

mixture into a frothy drink with a stirrer called a molinet.

The chocolate Cortés and other Spanish explorers took home to Spain was still a rather potent brew. No wonder the Spanish nobility quickly learned to sweeten it with honey and vanilla. For more than one hundred years the Spanish nobility kept their recipe to themselves. But it's hard to keep something as delicious as chocolate a secret for long. As Spanish royalty married kings and queens from other European countries, the word got out.

By the 1660 houses or cafés selling chocolate had sprung up throughout Europe.

Cocoa Beans

CACAO TREES grow close to the equator where the climate is warm all year round. You can also see them growing in greenhouses in such places as the Brooklyn Botanical Gardens and Hershey's Chocolate World.

All cocoa beans used in the United States, Canada, and Europe are imported. Two-thirds of the world's crop comes from Africa—Ghana, Ivory Coast, Nigeria, and Cameroon. Cacao plantations can also be found in Mexico, Trinidad, Costa Rica, Jamaica, and Haiti in Central America and New Guinea, Samoa, and Java in the Pacific. But the finest quality beans are grown in South America—Brazil, Ecuador, and Venezuela.

Because delicate cacao trees are unable to stand direct tropical sunlight, on most plantations they are planted in the shade of banana trees.

Since the growing season in the tropics is year round, ripe and unripe pods grow together on the same tree all year. But they are only harvested twice a year—in May, and October through November. Cocoa bean pickers, called tumbadores, look for yellow or orange streaks along the grooves of the pods, a sign of ripeness.

Cacao pods do not grow like apples and cherries, sprouting from stems at the ends of branches. Instead, cacao pods seem to pop out right from the trunk and thick main branches.

It is easy for the tumbadores, using machetes, to cut off the pods growing along the trunk. But they use long-handled knives to carefully snip the pods hanging from higher branches, so they won't break the fragile limbs or unripened pods.

People with baskets follow behind the tumbadores and gather the pods as they fall to the ground.

After the harvest, workers sitting in the shade of a tree or canopy crack open the ripe pods. Machetes whirling, these workers can split five hundred an hour.

CANADA

UNITED STATES

MEXICO

HAITI

JAMAICA

VENEZUELA

TRINIDAD

COSTA RICA

ECUADOR

SOUTH AMERICA

BRAZIL

EUROPE

AFRICA

GHANA

NIGER

IVORY COAST

CAMEROON

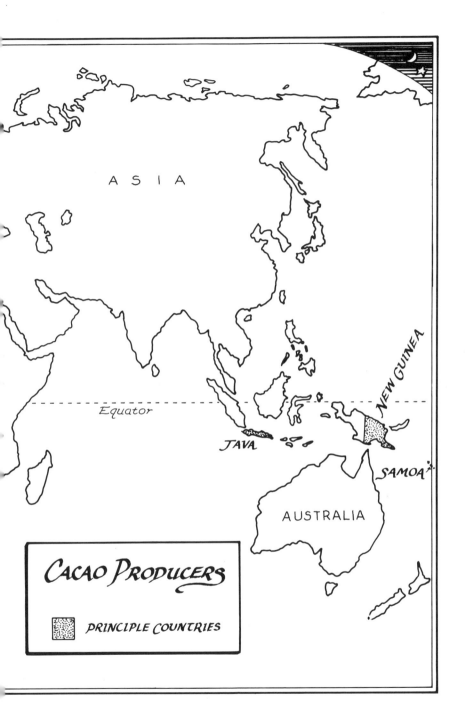

9

Pods on trees.

Inside the pods are what chocolate makers are after—twenty to fifty almond-shaped beans in a creamy pulp.

As soon as the ivory-colored beans are scooped from their shells, they react with oxygen in the air—a process called oxidation—and begin to change color. The beans are then heaped on the ground in large piles to ferment.

Fermentation is a natural process that changes apple juice to cider and cider to vinegar. Cocoa beans ferment when yeast and bacteria in the air act upon the sugar in the pulp, producing heat and acid, modifying the membranes of the beans. This chemical reaction inside the beans changes them so that their full flavor may be developed when the beans are roasted. During

10

fermentation the beans turn that distinctive, chocolaty reddish-brown color.

Workers cover the piles with banana leaves and palm fronds, turning them frequently so the beans ferment evenly.

In order to stop fermentation and guard against rotting, the beans must be dried. Usually, they are simply spread out in the sun for up to two weeks, mixed and turned often so they dry thoroughly. Sometimes machines are used, blowing hot air over trays of beans.

Once dried the beans are poured into burlap bags and hoisted onto ships bound for chocolate factories in the United States, Canada, and Europe.

Two cocoa bean pods (ruler shows scale). These mature pods will each contain 30–40 cocoa beans, the basis of all chocolate and confectionery products.

The size of actual beans.

Sacks of beans inside a railroad car.

12

When they arrive at port, the sacks are loaded onto railroad cars for the last leg of their journey.

At the plant the beans are fumigated to kill any insects that may have made cozy homes in the burlap sacks.

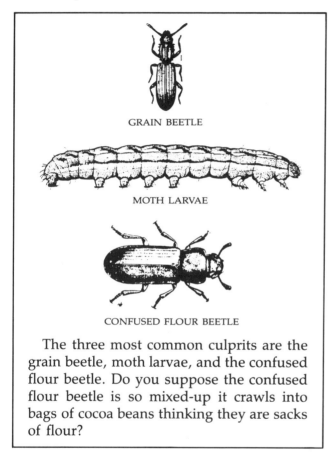

GRAIN BEETLE

MOTH LARVAE

CONFUSED FLOUR BEETLE

The three most common culprits are the grain beetle, moth larvae, and the confused flour beetle. Do you suppose the confused flour beetle is so mixed-up it crawls into bags of cocoa beans thinking they are sacks of flour?

The beans are then stored, either in tall stacks of burlap bags, or loose in towering silos.

Drawn from silos or emptied from bags, the beans are cleaned by sifting them through a series of sieves that filter out pebbles, dust, and other debris.

Hershey silos.

Making Chocolate

THE FIRST STEP in making chocolate is roasting the beans. This is important for developing their flavor. But if all the beans are roasted together, the little ones might get burned, while the big ones might not

14

be completely roasted. So first, the beans are sorted according to size.

Then, still in their shells, the beans are roasted in one of two ways: in a rotating drum where the beans tumble about inside a huge cylinder something like a clothes dryer, or in a continuous flow oven, where the beans travel on a conveyor belt through a tunnel heated to about 260 degrees C (500 degrees F). Either way, the result is the same—the beans are fully roasted. Then quickly, right out of the oven, they are cooled, capturing their peak flavor.

Heating also makes the shells easy to crack. So the beans are now ready for winnowing— separating the shells from the beans. Winnowing by hand takes too long for the millions of beans needed each day in a large chocolate factory, but machines would crush the hulls, leaving little pieces of shell mixed in with the beans. Instead, the beans are blown with tremendous force against a steel plate, to crack the hulls. The heavier beans, now called nibs, fall, while the lighter shells are blown up and away.

Every part of the cocoa bean is used. Vegetable fat is extracted from the shell, as well as theobromine, a stimulant used in some medicine. Shells are also used to make fertilizer and, ground up, they are added to cattle feed. Mulch from cocoa beans gives gardens a delicious, chocolaty fragrance.

Liquor mills at Wilbur.

Milling

NIBS USED to be ground by millstones, huge wheels chiseled out of rock, similar to those that were used to grind grain. Today, nibs are fed into pin mills, machines that have sets of disks with pins sticking from the face of each wheel.

Rotating in opposite directions, the two spinning disks quickly pulverize the nibs into a heavy syrup called liquor.

Since grinding wheat produces flour, you might expect grinding cocoa beans would make a powdery substance. However, cocoa butter, the fat found in cocoa beans, turns ground cocoa beans into a liquid paste—chocolate liquor.

Non-alcoholic, chocolate liquor is the basic ingredient of all chocolate products—cocoa, chocolate milk mix, milk chocolate, and all other chocolate candy except white chocolate.

Blending

IN ADDITION to roasting, chocolate makers create their distinctive flavors of chocolate by blending the chocolate liquors of different varieties of beans.

You may have noticed that not all chocolate tastes alike—Nestle's milk chocolate is slightly milder than Hershey's and Hershey's Special Dark is heartier than Hershey's kisses.

Connoisseurs of chocolate, those who really know and appreciate fine chocolate, are able to detect the slightest differences between chocolates.

Tasting differences among chocolates is a talent. Just as with other skills, such as music, art, and sports, some people possess more talent than others. How do chocolate makers know if someone is a good taster? They give that person a triangular taste test. The person is given three pieces of chocolate and asked to tell which two are alike. The test is repeated several times with different flavors of chocolate. Good tasters, of course, can tell every time which two chocolates are alike and which one is different.

Because milk chocolate tastes milder than dark chocolate, you probably think it is made from milder beans. That's not the case. Because milk chocolate contains a lot of milk, and less chocolate, liquor from robust or stronger-tasting beans is used. Bittersweet or dark chocolate uses much more liquor made from milder-tasting beans.

Chocolate makers often alter the taste of the chocolate to go with whatever is added to it. For example, a hearty chocolate that tastes just right with almonds might smother pecans. Therefore, a milder chocolate is used to make pecan bars.

Some coffee drinkers are so good at tasting that they can name the variety of bean used to brew the cup of coffee they are drinking. But don't be fooled by anyone claiming to know the blend of cocoa beans after eating some chocolate. It can't be done. Once blended, a batch of chocolate loses the particular flavors of the beans and acquires a new taste.

> *The flavor of chocolate may be described as floral, hammy, cheesy, chalky, woody, waxy, grainy, nutty, harsh, or mild.*

Sometimes, if a certain variety of bean is hard to get because of crop failure or some other problem, chocolate makers can adjust the blend—a little more liquor of one variety of bean to compensate for the liquor of another variety—and keep the flavor of the chocolate the same from batch to batch.

Recently, though, some South American countries have been making and exporting their own chocolate liquor rather than shipping the beans to the United States, Canada, and Europe. That shouldn't make much difference, but it might. Remember that once cocoa beans are made into liquor, it's impossible to tell what varieties of beans were used. Some chocolate companies feel they do not have full control over their chocolate making when they don't make their own liquor. They feel they can't be as sure they have top quality beans as when they process their own.

A cup of cocoa at bedtime.

20

Cocoa

A S LATE as the nineteenth century chocolate was still known only as a drink and tasted nothing like the instant chocolate milk you had for breakfast.

Ugh! In the 1800s, the fat of the roasted cocoa beans, called cocoa butter, often floated on top of the drink and people had to spoon it off.

The Aztecs added corn meal to reduce the fattiness of their chocolatl and to give it a more mellow taste. When the English stirred in potato starch to improve the taste, some enterprising merchants discovered that adding starches made the chocolate go further, increasing their profits. By the time of George III there were laws to keep chocolate pure. Unfortunately, nobody paid much attention to them. But today the Food and Drug Administration (FDA) states exactly how much chocolate liquor and cocoa butter chocolate products must contain. Unsweetened, bitter, or baking chocolate, the kind used for cooking, has the most cocoa butter and chocolate liquor. Semisweet chocolate, also used for cooking, has a little sugar added. Dark chocolate, which you eat, has more sugar added. And milk chocolate contains milk and even more sugar.

A chocolate maker from Holland, C.J. van Houten, was interested in making a more pleasant-tasting drink by removing the cocoa butter. He didn't want to do it by adding other ingredients, such as corn meal, to soak up the fat. That would have made the drink thicker and less pure. Instead, van Houten invented the first cocoa press to squeeze out the cocoa butter.

Cocoa butter is used in the manufacture of suntan lotion, soap, and moisturizers.

Tins of cocoa.

Cocoa is still produced almost this same way. Chocolate liquor is pumped into cylinders and forced through screens, filtering out the cocoa butter. What's left is a brown flaky powder—cocoa.

But van Houten didn't stop there. Still searching for a more mellow, a more digestible chocolate drink, he discovered a way of neutralizing the acids within cocoa. Through a process known as "Dutching," van Houten added alkalis to cancel the acids, making cocoa even milder.

23

Milk Chocolate

I N 1847 the English made the first chocolate to eat, and in 1876 two Swiss chocolate makers, Daniel Peter and Henri Nestlé created milk chocolate.

To make milk chocolate, you need milk—and plenty of it. More than 50,000 cows are necessary to give 1,000,000 pounds of milk, delivered fresh to a chocolate plant every day.

Would you believe, a cow?

Sugar is added to milk, then the mixture is dried until it looks like taffy. Chocolate liquor and this taffylike milk are kneaded together to make a flaky cake called crumb.

Do you remember the cocoa butter left over from making cocoa? Most cocoa butter is mixed with the crumb, creating a thick chocolate paste.

Refiners

Refining

ONE MEASURE of fine chocolate is its smoothness. The smaller the particles of chocolate, the smoother it is.

To make chocolate smoother the thick paste is fed into a series of five rollers, one stacked on top of another, rotating in opposite directions. With each successive roller turning faster than the one below it, the paste is picked up and ground finer and finer.

In the vat below the bottom roller, the chocolate appears grainy, as if it were mixed with fine sand. But the chocolate leaving the top roller is creamy smooth, with particles of chocolate no bigger than 30 to 50 thousandths of a millimeter.

Chocolate leaving the last roll of the refiner.

Below the waterfall (and this was the most astonishing sight of all), a whole mass of enormous glass pipes were dangling down into the river from somewhere high up in the ceiling! They really were *enormous*, those pipes. . . . And because they were made of glass, you could see the liquid flowing and bubbling along inside them, and above the noise of the waterfall, you could hear the never-ending suck-suck-sucking sound of the pipes as they did their work.

* * *

"There" cried Mr. Wonka, dancing up and down and pointing his gold-topped cane at the great brown river. "It's *all* chocolate! Every drop of that river is hot melted chocolate of the finest quality. The *very* finest quality. There's enough chocolate in there to fill *every* bathtub in the *entire* country! *And* all the swimming pools as well! Isn't it *terrific*? And just look at my pipes! They suck up the chocolate and carry it away to all the other rooms in the factory where it is needed! Thousands of gallons an hour, my dear children! Thousands and thousands of gallons!"

* * *

"The waterfall is *most* important!" Mr. Wonka went on. "It mixes the chocolate! It churns it up! It pounds it and beats it! It makes it light and frothy! No other factory in the world mixes its chocolate by waterfall!. . ."
Charlie and the Chocolate Factory by Roald Dahl

*Conching machines
at Hershey.*

Of course, that's not exactly what a modern chocolate factory looks like. But Charlie Bucket and the other children would be just as impressed in a real plant, especially with the conching room.

That's where the finely ground but still grainy-looking chocolate is slowly stirred in vats about as big as twenty-four bathtubs!

Back and forth, back and forth, back and forth, heavy granite rollers push and pull the creamy smooth chocolate in granite-bottom basins, almost like your using a painter's roller to stir chocolate in a long pan.

As waves of luscious chocolate roll forward, you might be tempted to dip your finger into one of these gigantic mixing bowls for one little taste. But you better not. The stirring creates friction that heats the chocolate to 120–190 degrees F.

> *Some say the word conch comes from the Spanish* concha, *meaning shell, the kind you find at the seashore and put to your ear to "hear" the ocean. Others claim the word is French for shell-like trough.*

Conching not only dissolves any lumps but it also makes the chocolate smooth, covering each tiny particle with a thin coating of cocoa butter. To develop its fullest flavor, some milk chocolate is conched for seventy-two hours. That's three full days!

To make certain that each batch has exactly the proper proportion of ingredients, especially cocoa butter, technicians draw samples of chocolate and take them to the laboratory to be analyzed. In this way, each batch of a particular kind of chocolate, say Hershey Kisses, is guaranteed to taste like all others.

Samples of milk chocolate are collected by quality assurance technicians for laboratory testing.

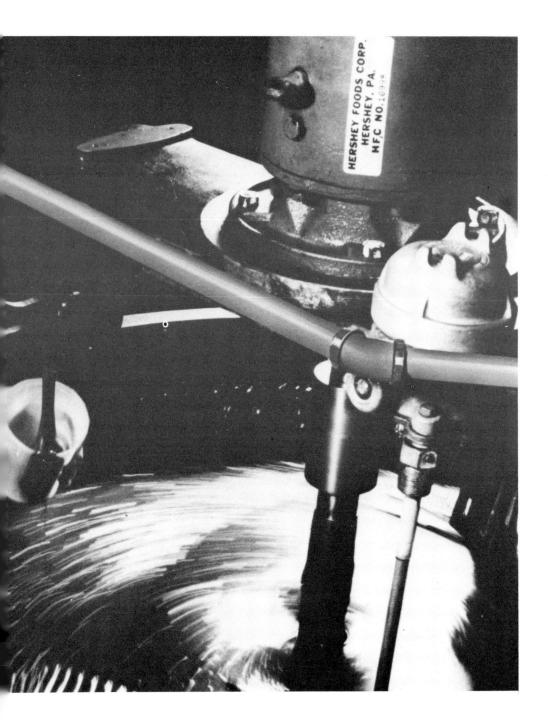

Empty bar molds on a conveyor belt enter the depositor on one of Hershey's milk chocolate bar lines.

Chocolate Cools
Its Temper

PERHAPS you have heard of tempering in the making of steel. By cooling molten steel, reheating it, and cooling it again, steel is made stronger.

Chocolate, too, is tempered, making it more stable—less likely to melt on store shelves.

As I said before the chocolate is quite warm—between 120 degrees and 190 degrees F (49 degrees to 88 degrees C) when it comes from the conching machine. This liquid chocolate is poured into large kettles that have linings filled with water. The water circulates around the kettle to cool the chocolate to between 82 degrees and 84 degrees F (28 degrees to 29 degrees C). This cooling creates crystals in the cocoa butter. Developing the proper crystals is the key to shelf life, the time chocolate can remain on store shelves. Tiny crystals are the most stable. Larger crystals tend to break down more easily. So after

A Wilbur mold

cooling, the chocolate is reheated slightly to eliminate the large crystals.

Now the chocolate is ready to be poured into molds with the brand name of the chocolate bar written across the bottom of the mold, backward. That's so you'll be able to read the brand name when the chocolate bar is lifted from its mold.

If the chocolate bar has nuts—peanuts, almonds, or pecans—or crisped rice, these are dropped into the molds with liquid chocolate.

Rocky Road

IN THEIR MOLDS the liquid chocolate bars go on a bouncy, bumpy ride to shake out any air bubbles that may have formed. Back on a smooth road, they are rushed into the cooling tunnel where the liquid chocolate becomes a solid candy bar.

But before being wrapped, the chocolate bar must past the inspector, who carefully examines each one, checking for cracks, air bubbles, or uneven distribution of nuts.

Using a vacuum hose, she lifts out these less-than-perfect bars.

GOOD GRIEF! What happens to this absolutely good chocolate?

Some of these broken bars are served, free, to the chocolate plant and office workers. That's the best part of working in a chocolate factory.

But in a day's time there are more broken

Milk chocolate bar line inspection—imperfectly molded bars are rejected.

pieces than the chocolate workers can eat, so most of this chocolate is recycled—remelted and poured into molds again.

With so much free chocolate around, are chocolate workers fat? In three different chocolate plants, I noticed very few overweight chocolate workers. Most looked quite normal. But one woman did confess that she had to learn to control her snacking.

35

Wrapping machine

Having passed the test, the chocolate bars move along to the packaging room. Although some boxed chocolates are wrapped by hand, most chocolate bars are machine wrapped.

As each bar is gently dumped from its mold, ribbons of colorful wrappers stream from machines. Quickly the chocolate bars are bundled in shiny foil and slipped into paper sleeves bearing their brand name. Every minute six hundred milk chocolate bars shoot from machines into a tray. There, workers gather them and package the bars, first in small cardboard boxes, then in large cartons for shipment to stores.

Boxed chocolate

Boxed Chocolates

IF YOU HEAR people talking about "boxed chocolates," they're referring to chocolate candy pieces packaged in fancy boxes.

Usually, these pieces have centers of creams, caramels, cherries, or nuts. Some box lids tell what's inside. Other times you can tell by the swirl on top—M for marshmallow, C for caramel, and so on. Often you are left to guess. Isn't it a surprise biting into the coconut-filled piece you thought was a chocolate-covered cherry!

Luxury or designer chocolates are expensive boxed chocolates. That's because the process for making them takes more time and also because they are made from the finest chocolate.

One taste will tell the difference. Try a piece of ordinary boxed chocolate. It's delicious, right.

Now try a piece of luxury chocolate. Pause a moment to let the rich chocolate pamper your taste buds. That's unbelievably, marvelously, supremely, sublimely delicious chocolate! That's the difference.

Luxury chocolates are sometimes placed in fancy boxes called ballotins, French for small package.

Most designer chocolate is remanufactured. That is, a chocolate company makes huge

FACING PAGE:
*Large bars, which later
will be melted at a boxed
chocolate plant.*

batches of chocolate. Sometimes the chocolate is made into enormous chocolate bars, which are bought by the boxed-chocolate company, and then melted.

Other times, batches of liquid chocolate are shipped in heated tank trucks that keep the chocolate melted and warm, even on the coldest days.

Designer chocolates

Fruits and Nuts

HOW DO THEY get all those fruits and nuts into the middle of chocolates? In the small candy kitchens, ladies hand dip centers into melted chocolate to coat them.

In a corner of the luxury chocolate plant, some women sit at a small table absorbed in conversation. With quick fingers these ladies sort through thousands of shelled walnuts, making sure each is perfectly formed, sifting out any shell fragments.

Later, these walnuts will be enrobed, a process similar to hand-dipping. As the walnuts travel on a conveyor belt, nozzles squirt them with a coating or two of chocolate.

Other designer chocolates are made in molded shells. A machine called a depositer squeezes liquid chocolate into half-shell molds. The molds are first flipped upside down to drain off excess chocolate, which is caught in trays below and recycled.

FACING PAGE:
A worker hand-dips pretzels into chocolate.

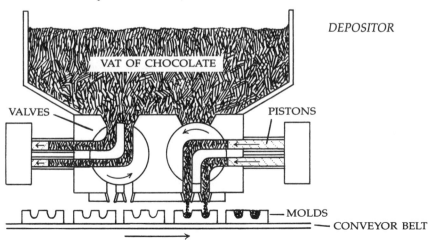

DEPOSITOR

These half-shell molds are then rushed into cooling towers where the chocolate hardens. Now they are ready to be filled with the creamiest creams, tastiest fruits, and crunchiest nuts.

The two half-shell molds are joined together by heating the edges of the chocolate shells and then folding one half-shell onto another. Again, the molds travel into cooling towers where the liquid chocolate around the seams of the candy hardens, cementing the two halves.

Single mold chocolates travel upside down to be filled. After filling, the bottoms are covered with chocolate before they are cooled.

Godiva molds

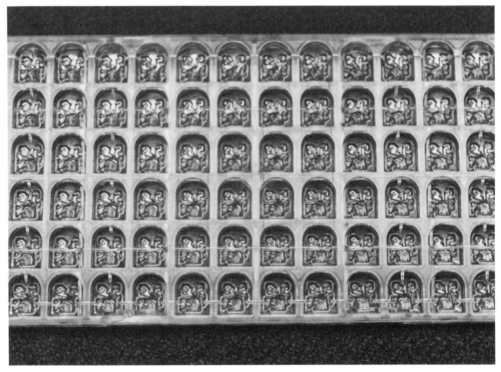

Half-shell chocolates.
Notice the seams on half-shells.

Easter bunnies are made by dropping liquid chocolate into a double mold that is clamped shut. The mold rotates so the chocolate inside the molds rolls into every nook and crevice of the hollow bunny.

Since cocoa butter shrinks when it cools, the chocolate is slightly smaller after it has been cooled and falls out of its mold. Nevertheless, a machine vibrates each mold gently, nudging those bunnies too lazy to hop out on their own.

Truffles

PERHAPS the most heavenly of the luxury chocolates are truffles. Surely, they are the most expensive luxury chocolates. These treats are created from rich dairy cream and whipped into an airy chocolaty delight.

Chocolate truffles have nothing to do with the European delicacy—an underground fungus, snorted out by trained pigs and served in salads.

A truffle

You may recall that imperfect candy bars, those with cracks, bubbles, or minor flaws, are recycled—melted and remade into new candy bars. But with truffles and luxury chocolates, the creamy, fruity centers cannot be separated from the chocolate. Some with minor flaws are sold as seconds to chocolate workers. But some pieces are such gooey gobs, they aren't fit for anybody, especially if they've fallen onto the floor.

Fortunately, just down the valley from the chocolate plant is a farm where some of the luckiest, most privileged pigs in the world live. Can you imagine those happy hogs, topping off their dinner of slops with exquisite chocolates?

Cut in half

What's in a Name?

CHOCOLATE comes from the Aztec, chocolatl, sometimes spelled xocoatl. Some etymologists—people who study where words come from—believe that *latl* meant water and *choco* described the sound of mixing ground-up beans in water—choco, choco, choco. Others think chocolatl meant *bitter water*, which is probably exactly how their early chocolate drink tasted.

The Spanish, trying to imitate the Aztecs, said, "Chocolate" (Cho-co-LAH-tay). When the French discovered the Spaniard's secret, they called it "Chocolat" (Sho-co-LAH). Taking the exotic drink across the English Channel, the British said, variously, "Chocolata," "Jocolatte," or "Chockelet." When this, now more pleasant-tasting drink traveled back across the Atlantic, the Americans gave it the familiar name, "Chocolate."

Cacao usually refers to the tree or pods. Cocoa describes the bean or the dry powder your mother uses in cooking.

Truffle-eating pigs!

Blooming Chocolate

HAVE YOU EVER taken the wrapper off a chocolate bar and discovered it was covered with a thin white film? Maybe you thought it was spoiled. Actually, the chocolate was affected by what is called "bloom."

Bloom occurs when the temperature where the chocolate is kept is too high, over 70 degrees

Enjoying chocolate.

F (26 degrees C). A small amount of cocoa butter separates and works its way to the surface. When the temperature falls, this cocoa butter crystalizes, forming the powdery white coating called "bloom." Proper tempering makes bloom less likely.

There is nothing wrong with "blooming" chocolate. It may have lost some of its smoothness, but otherwise it tastes just fine. With proper storage, bloom can be avoided.

Enjoying Chocolate: *Recipes*

Hot Chocolate for Those Frosty Evenings

1 heaping teaspoon of cocoa
1 ½ heaping teaspoons of sugar (or 1 bag Nutrasweet)
2 tablespoons of hot water
a little less than a cup of milk
½ teaspoon of vanilla
one marshmallow

In a saucepan mix cocoa and sugar and hot water. Stir until it boils.

Add milk and reduce heat. Do not boil!

Whisk (beat with wire or rotary beater) for about 15 seconds until foamy. Whisking keeps skin from forming, dissolves any small lumps, and develops flavor.

Finally, add marshmallow, drink and enjoy.

CHOCOLATE CAKE
by Nina Payne

Chocolate cake
Chocolate cake
that's the one
I'll help you make
Flour soda
salt are sifted
butter sugar
cocoa lifted
by the eggs
then mix the whole
grease the pans
I'll lick the bowl
Chocolate caked
chocolate caked
that's what I'll be
when it's baked.

Milk Chocolate Bar Cake

8 ounces of milk chocolate bars, broken into pieces
  (That's a little less than 6 (1.4 oz.) regular milk
  chocolate bars.)
¼ cup butter or margarine
1 ⅔ cups boiling water
2 ⅓ cups unsifted all-purpose flour
2 cups packed light brown sugar
2 teaspoons baking soda
1 teaspoon salt
2 eggs
½ cup sour cream
1 teaspoon vanilla

Combine milk chocolate bar pieces, butter (or margarine), and boiling water in medium-size mixing bowl; stir until chocolate is melted.

Combine flour, brown sugar, baking soda, and salt in large mixing bowl; gradually add chocolate mixture, beating until thoroughly blended.

Blend in eggs, sour cream, and vanilla; beat one minute on medium speed.

Pour into greased and floured 13 by 9-inch pan. Bake at 350 degrees F for 35 to 40 minutes or until cake tester comes out clean. Cool completely; frost as desired.

Makes 8 to 10 servings.

This cake really tastes like a milk chocolate bar.

CHOCOLATE MILK
by Ron Padgett

Oh God! It's great
to have someone fix you
chocolate milk
and to appreciate their doing it!
Even as they stir it
in the kitchen
your mouth is going crazy
for the chocolate milk!
The wonderful chocolate milk!

Choice Moist Chocolate Cake

3 cups flour
2 cups sugar
1 teaspoon baking soda
¾ cup cocoa
Mix in bowl.

Add:
2 teaspoons vinegar
2 teaspoons vanilla
1 cup oil

Pour 2 cups water over all.
Beat until smooth.
Pour batter into 9 by 13-inch sheet pan.
Bake at 350 degrees F for 35 minutes.

This cake is truly moist and it's surprisingly easy to make. Any young person, under a parent's supervision, should have no trouble baking it.

Microwave Fudge

3 cups semisweet or milk chocolate chips
1 14-ounce can sweetened condensed milk (such as Eagle Brand)
¼ cup butter or margarine
1½ teaspoons vanilla
1 cup chopped walnuts

Place all ingredients except nuts in large mixing bowl. (Be sure the bowl can be used in a microwave oven.) Microwave at Medium (50%) until chocolate chips are melted (3 to 5 minutes). Stir once or twice during cooking.

Stir in nuts.

Pour into well-greased, 8 by 8-inch square baking dish. Refrigerate until set.

If you do not have a microwave oven, place the ingredients (except walnuts) into a double boiler. You can make your own double boiler by pouring the ingredients into a saucepan and placing that saucepan in a larger saucepan partly filled with water.

Cook over medium heat for about 15 to 20 minutes (until all the ingredients are melted and evenly mixed).

Stir frequently.

Turn off heat and stir in nuts.

Pour into well-greased, 8 by 8-inch baking dish. Refrigerate until set.

You simply cannot buy a smoother, sweeter, better tasting fudge anywhere.

A GREAT MOMENT IN CHOCOLATE

In 1920, Otto Schnering, owner of the Curtiss Candy Company, introduced a candy bar, Baby Ruth, in honor of President Grover Cleveland's daughter who, as an infant, had captured the hearts of the nation.

As a publicity stunt, a chartered plane flew over Pittsburgh and dropped thousands of Baby Ruth bars, each gently floating to earth under its own parachute.

Brownies

½ cup butter or margarine
1 cup sugar
1 teaspoon vanilla
2 eggs
2 one-ounce squares unsweetened chocolate, melted
and cooled
½ cup sifted all-purpose flour
½ chopped walnuts

Beat butter, sugar, and vanilla until creamy.
(This may take a while.)
Beat in eggs.
Blend in chocolate.
Stir in flour and nuts.
Bake in greased 8 by 8 by 2-inch pan at 325
degrees F, 30 to 35 minutes.
Cool and cut into squares.

These rich, chewy brownies make a great after-
school snack.

Chocolate Fondue: A Great Party Idea

For chocolate lovers, there is no end to the
foods that can be dipped into chocolate—straw-
berries, pretzels, and animal crackers taste sen-
sational this way.

At your next party, instead of the usual mun-
chies, why not set out some of your favorite
treats and a pot of melted chocolate.

But first, here are a few hints about melting
chocolate:

Just placing chocolate in a pan and turning
on the burner may scorch the chocolate, giving

it a burnt taste. Too high heat can cause milk chocolate to become stiff, like taffy.

A good way to melt chocolate is to boil water in a shallow saucepan. Then, in a smaller pot, break up the chocolate into pieces. Once the water boils, remove the saucepan from the heat and place the pot with the chocolate in it. When the chocolate is melted, stir for smoothness.

Be careful not to allow any water to get into the chocolate. That can also make it stiff. But if that should happen, add a teaspoon of corn oil and stir.

Another way to melt chocolate is in the oven. In a pan break the chocolate into small pieces. Place the pan in the oven at 110 degrees F (45 degrees C) for about an hour. This is just like leaving your chocolate bar in the sun on a summer's day.

Storing and Keeping Chocolate

CHOCOLATE is best stored away from direct sunlight in a cool area—between 55 and 65 degrees F (12 and 18 degrees) never above 70 degrees F (21 degrees C).

Under proper conditions, dark chocolate may be stored for a few months. Milk chocolate can be kept for four months, but boxed chocolates should be eaten more quickly.

To keep chocolate longer you should freeze

it. Just be sure the chocolate has a chance to thaw before eating, otherwise, it may be brittle and not as tasty.

Because chocolate absorbs odors of other food, it is best to wrap chocolate in an air-tight plastic bag. Otherwise, your delicious chocolate could taste a little like last night's fish.

THE GREENHOUSE EFFECT

On a mild, sunny spring day be careful about leaving your chocolate in a parked car. Sunshine streaming through the windows gets trapped inside the car. After a while, say a few hours of shopping, this sunshine can heat up your car. Scientists call this the greenhouse effect. When you open your car door, you may notice that it's very warm inside and that your chocolate has turned into a brown puddle.

Places to Visit

IF YOU WANT to know more about chocolate firsthand, there are two interesting places to visit—Hershey's Chocolate World in Hershey, Pennsylvania, and Wilbur Chocolate's Candy Americana Museum in Lititz, Pennsylvania. Both are free and are located within a forty-five minute drive of one another.

A special bonus greets visitors to these chocolate towns—a rich, chocolaty aroma wafts past your nose. Lining Cocoa Avenue, the main

Hershey lampposts

street in Hershey, are lampposts shaped like Hershey Kisses, alternating between silver (wrapped) and brown (chocolate).

In this small valley stands the world's largest chocolate plant, founded in 1900 by Milton Hershey.

Not far from the plant is Chocolate World where visitors can climb aboard automated carts that travel past huge dioramas that tell the story of chocolate. At journey's end you can visit the chocolate soda fountain. There, beside a small tropical rain forest that includes real banana and cacao trees, you can enjoy an ice cream sundae lavished with thick chocolate syrup.

A short drive through the beautiful Pennsylvania Dutch countryside takes you to the quiet town of Lititz, home of the Wilbur Chocolate Company.

Wilbur may not be as well-known as Hershey, even though it makes a full line of creamy, mellow milk and dark chocolate, including Wilbur Buds. But you've probably eaten Wilbur chocolate and not known it. That's because Wilbur makes chocolate for a lot of other chocolate candy companies.

At the front of the plant is the Candy Americana Museum which features old-fashioned chocolate making utensils, molds, and machines as well as labels, boxes, and tins from many turn-of-the-century brands of chocolate and cocoa.

There is a life-size replica of an old-time candy kitchen and at the other end of the museum is a modern kitchen where delectable chocolate confections are concocted on the spot just for you.

A valentine box of chocolates.

Chocolate and Love

A FAVORITE GIFT of lovers on Valentine's Day is a box of chocolates. That's no accident. Chocolate and love have been linked together for centuries. Montezuma supposedly drank more than fifty cups of chocolate a day, thinking the drink would make him feel more passionate.

Believing chocolate sparked one's passions, Joan Franc Rauch of Vienna suggested in 1624 that monks should not be allowed to drink chocolate.

61

Actually, there is a chemical in chocolate—phenylethylamine—which is also produced by the brain when you're in love. Some people even claim they taste chocolate when they're in love. But don't worry, eating chocolate probably will not cause you to fall in love with the first person you see.

MOTHER'S VALENTINE CHOCOLATE
by Jack Prelutsky

I bought a box of chocolate hearts,
a present for my mother,
they looked so good I tasted one,
and then I tried another.

They both were so delicious
that I ate another four,
and then another couple,
and then a half dozen more.

I couldn't seem to stop myself,
I nibbled on and on,
before I knew what happened
all the chocolate hearts were gone.

I felt a little guilty,
I was stuffed down to my socks,
I ate my mother's valentine . . .
I hope she likes the box.

Mock Chocolate

SO-CALLED diet chocolate is sweetened with sorbitol (Nutrasweet) instead of sugar. Although small lettering on the label reads, "Not for weight control," the "diet chocolate" contains only 24 calories per ounce compared to 147 calories in regular milk chocolate. Trouble is, the chocolate tastes washed out, not very chocolaty at all.

Carob is not chocolate. It is made from the ground-up fruit of an evergreen tree found in the Mediterranean. When mixed with fats and other ingredients, its taste comes close to that of chocolate. But not close enough. It does not smell like chocolate and its texture is not like chocolate—it's much too grainy. But it does look like chocolate!

ANOTHER GREAT MOMENT IN CHOCOLATE

The original script for the movie, *E.T. The Extra-Terrestrial*, called for Elliott to leave a trail of M&Ms for E.T. to follow. Unfortunately, the people at Mars, who make M&Ms, didn't think this film would be a hit, and not wanting to be associated with a flop, said, "No, thanks," to the movie-makers.

Happily, the folks at Hershey Foods jumped at the chance to have E.T. follow a path of Reese's Pieces.

Often carob bars are sold in health food stores with the claim that they are "natural." But if "natural" means no artificial ingredients, then real chocolate must also be considered "natural."

If you are one of those unfortunate people who is allergic to chocolate, carob makes a sensible substitute.

Chocolate Etiquette

TRY TO BE NEAT.

Be careful not to get any chocolate on your clothing.

Take small bites. It's less messy and your taste buds will have more bites to savor. Wolfing down fine chocolate defeats the pleasure of eating it. Take your time.

If your hands become chocolaty, do not shake hands with someone (unless they have chocolaty hands, too). Do not scratch your head or wipe chocolaty hands on your shirt or pants.

If, by accident, you should get some chocolate on your clothing, here's how to get it out. Since chocolate contains a lot of cocoa butter, it has an oil base that must be broken down. Ammonia and water as well as other household detergents dissolve the oil so it may be rinsed away with water. For stubborn stains you may need to tamp (pat) the spot with a cloth saturated with a cleaner.

Girl neatly eating chocolate.

Girl messily eating chocolate.

THE REASON I LIKE CHOCOLATE
by Nikki Giovanni

The reason I like chocolate
is I can lick my fingers
and nobody tells me I'm not polite.

CHOCOLATE
by Russell Hoban

Why did I forget the chocolate
I was saving in my pocket
When my blue jeans went into the washer?

Food Value

FOOD	WATER %	FOOD ENERGY calories	PROTEIN gm	FAT gm	CARBO-HYDRATE gm	CALCIUM mg
APPLES *Raw, commercial varieties:* *Whole good quality (refuse: core and stem, 8%)* *Fruit, 3¼ in. diam.* *1 Apple—230 Grams*	84.4	123	.4	1.3	30.7	15
MILK CHOCOLATE *Plain 1 oz.—28 Grams*	.9	147	2.2	9.2	16.1	65
RAISINS, NATURAL, SEEDLESS TYPE *1 oz.—28 Grams*	18.0	82	.7	.1	21.9	18
PEANUTS *Roasted, salted—1 oz.—28 Grams*	1.6	166	7.4	14.1	5.3	21
YOGURT *Made from partially skimmed milk* *1 cup—245 Grams*	89.0	123	8.3	4.2	12.7	294
ICE CREAM *1 Cup (8 fl. oz.) regular* *(approx. 10% fat)—133 Grams*	63.2	257	6.0	14.1	27.7	194

Chocolate Myths

Myth #1 Chocolate causes cavities.

According to the American Dental Association, researchers have found that chocolate helps fight tooth decay. Chocolate contains a protein that blocks plaque.

# of Chocolate

PHOS-PHORUS mg	IRON mg	SODIUM gm	POTASSIUM gm	A VALUE gm	THIAMINE mg	RIBOFLAVIN mg	NIACIN mg	ASCORBIC ACID mg
21	.6	2	233	190	.06	.04	.2	8
65	.3	27	109	80	.02	.10	.1	Trace
29	1.0	8	216	10	.03	.02	.1	Trace
114	.6	119	191	—	.09	.04	4.9	0
230	.1	125	350	170	.10	.44	.2	2
153	.1	84	241	590	.05	.28	.1	1

Actually, it is the sugar, not chocolate, that is converted into acid by bacteria in the mouth, that causes cavities. Also, tiny particles of food can cling to teeth and decay. Cocoa butter in chocolate helps rinse these particles from the mouth, reducing the chance of cavities.

Myth #2 Chocolate is fattening.

Chocolate contains no more calories than yogurt, almost no salt, and no cholesterol. Chocolate does contain many important nutrients, including calcium, protein, and riboflavin (one of the B vitamins).

Myth #3 Chocolate causes pimples.

For a long time people believed that chocolate caused acne (pimples). Then some doctors gave chocolate to adolescents with acne. For some, their acne did get worse. But for others, it stayed the same or got better. This experiment led doctors to believe that eating chocolate does not effect acne one way or the other. So if you're a teenager, that's good news.

Myth #4 White chocolate is pure chocolate.

White chocolate has no chocolate liquor, the basic ingredient of chocolate. Rather, it is made with only cocoa butter, sugar, and milk. Because it contains no chocolate liquor, white chocolate is not real chocolate.

Myth #5 Paraffin is added to chocolate.

Some people believe that paraffin is added to chocolate. This is not true. You cannot digest paraffin. Therefore, it is against government regulations for chocolate companies to add paraffin to chocolate.

Myth #6 Sugar gives chocolate its "quick energy."

Actually, caffeine and theobromine, both stimulants, are found naturally in the cocoa bean. Chocolate, however, contains only about one-tenth to one-twenty-fifth of the caffeine

present in coffee. Moreover, theobromine affects muscles, not nerves, so you don't feel "nervous" or jittery from eating a lot of chocolate, the way some people do after drinking a lot of coffee.

Myth #7 European chocolates are better.

Some people think that Europeans produce superior chocolate. They may get this notion because European chocolate makers export their finest chocolates. America's finest chocolates compare quite favorably with the best European kinds.

Foil covered novelty chocolates.

Jokes

Why is chocolate ice cream like a race horse?

The more you lick it, the faster it goes.

What do you get when you cross an alligator with a Hershey bar?

A Chocodile.

What is an elklike animal that runs through a chocolate factory?

A Chocolate Mousse

What's brown and silver and runs in the heat?

A chocolate candy bar.

What do you say if you fall into a vat of chocolate?

Fire! Fire! Because nobody would believe you if you called, Chocolate! Chocolate!

Why did the hippopotamus stand on the marshmallow?

So he wouldn't fall into the hot chocolate

Bibliography

Borror, Donald and Dwight DeLong. *An Introduction to the Study of Insects*. Holt, Rinehart & Winston, 1964.

Boynton, Sandra. *Chocolate: The Consuming Passion*. New York: Workman Publishing Company, 1982.

Broekel, Ray. *The Chocolate Chronicles*. Lombard, Illinois: Wallace-Homestead, 1985.

――――. "Land of the Candy Bar," *American Heritage*. Vol. 37, No. 6, October-November, 1986. pp. 74-80.

"Chocolate bars," *Consumer Reports*, Vol. 51, No. 11, Nov., 1986. pp. 696–701.

Cook, L. Russell. *Chocolate Production and Use*. New York: Books for Industry, Inc., 1972.

Dahl, Roald. *Charlie and the Chocolate Factory*, Illustrated by Joseph Schindelman. Knopf, 1964.

Galvin, Ruth Mehrteens. "Sybaritic to some, sinful to others, but how sweet it is!" *The Smithsonian*. February, 1986, pp. 54–66.

Hearn, Michael Patrick. *The Chocolate Book*. New York: Caedmon, 1983.

Hershey's Chocolate Treasury. New York: Golden Press, 1984.

Kolpas, Norman. *The Chocolate Lover's Companion*. Twickenham, England: The Felix Gluck Press, Ltd., 1977.

Marcus, Adrianne. *The Chocolate Bible*. New York: Putnam, 1979.

Mitgutsch, Ali. *From Cacao Bean to Chocolate*. Minneapolis: Carolrhoda, 1975.

Morton, Marcia and Frederic. *Chocolate*. Crown, 1986

Nolan, Susan, *Hershey's Chocolate and Cocoa Cookbook*. Milwaukee, Wisconsin: Ideals Publishing Corporation, 1982

Rinzler, Carol Ann. *The Book of Chocolate*. New York: St. Martin's Press, 1977.

Index

EDUCATION